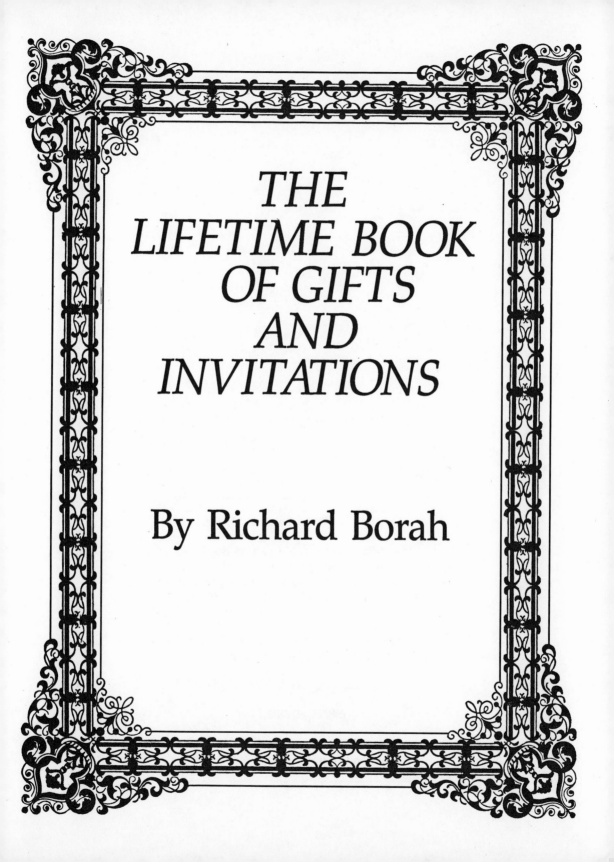

THE
LIFETIME BOOK
OF GIFTS
AND
INVITATIONS

By Richard Borah

Published by Leicester House, Ltd., 624 Nutley Place, No. Woodmere, New York

Library of Congress Catalog Card No. 80–81453

ISBN 0–918252–01–6

Designed by Nicola Mazzella
Cover and Form Design by Robin Lazarus

CONTENTS

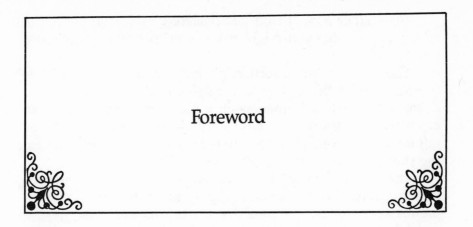

Foreword

This book has been written to help you with any problems you might have when giving and receiving gifts and invitations. Our lives are marked by momentous occasions when we extend invitations and accept the offerings of those close to us. At other times we receive an invitation and are obliged to confer some token of our affection upon the sender. Many problems may arise for both the host and the guest at these times. The host may be unsure about:

Who it is proper to invite (or not invite) to a particular function?

How and where to keep an organized list of those invited and whether they have accepted or not?

How and where to keep a record of who gave which gift so that he can write proper thank-you notes?

What type of invitation should be sent for a formal, semi-formal or informal affair?

The guest may be concerned with:

What is an appropriate gift for a particular occasion?

When is money a proper or improper gift?

How expensive a gift should be given?

When is it unnecessary to give a gift?

Where will he keep a record of the gift he gives someone so he can avoid giving someone the same gift twice?

The Lifetime Book of Gifts and Invitations has been written to relieve any doubts you might have about the answers to these questions.

This book contains a section in which you may keep complete records of invitations given and received as well as a place for keeping complete information on gifts. In this text there is an extensive discussion of the proper criteria to use when selecting a gift for an occasion. This may prove to be an invaluable guide for the young or inexperienced gift-giver.

The section "Thirty Vital Questions and Answers About Gifts and Invitations" covers a wide range of unwritten rules concerning the act of giving and receiving invitations and gifts.

I hope this book proves to be a useful and pleasurable experience for you and an important addition to your family library.

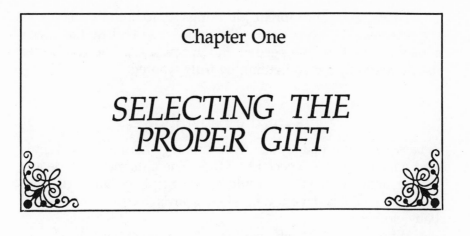

Chapter One

SELECTING THE PROPER GIFT

"If the man at the door has no shoes, you have not to consider whether you could procure him a paint-box."
—*Emerson*

Joyous and important dates in our lives are often highlighted by the gifts we receive from family and friends. The first time a child rips away the wrapping paper to reveal a longed-for doll or baseball mitt is the beginning of a life-long process that will never lose its appeal. People of all ages and personalities love to receive gifts.

Selecting a gift, however, is not as simple as receiving one. Care must be taken that what we are giving is what the recipient desires and not something suited to our own tastes. Sometimes the most well-meaning person will give the most inappropriate present. A rich man buying his poorer friend's wife an expensive gift can create an embarrassing and unpleasant situation.

There are times when our eagerness to show affection blinds us to the more sensible side of gift-giving. Of course the act of giving a gift is a personal one, unique to the relationship between the bestower and the recipient. It is not the purpose of this text to tell you what are the "right" gifts or the "wrong" gifts for any particular person. What is proposed in this section are some guidelines which may aid you in choosing the most appropriate and well-received gift for an occasion.

Choosing an appropriate gift brings joy to both the giver and the receiver. The giver enjoys the knowledge that he has given something that will be needed and appreciated. The receiver is happy to finally get something he truly wanted.

Gifts for the Baby Shower

A baby shower is usually a fairly informal gathering of the friends and relatives of the expectant mother. The gifts may include any of the items a newborn would need. Some popular gifts are blankets, mobiles, layettes, bassinets, carriage covers, rattles and baby clothes.

When attending a shower for a child not yet born the clothes should be of neutral colors. It would be unwise to buy pink pajamas for what might be a baby boy. Yellow is a safe favorite in this situation.

If you choose to buy a toy for the baby (e.g., a rattle), be careful that it is:

soft and rounded (no sharp edges)
light enough so that a baby would not hurt himself if he hit the toy against his head
large enough not to be swallowed
clear and bright in color
easy to hold (in the case of a rattle).

I should mention that people of the Jewish faith traditionally do not purchase anything for a child until it has been born. To do so is considered bad luck. Obviously it would be tactless to send gifts to a Jewish couple before their child is born. Often in this religion a baby shower will be held after the birth.

If a couple sends you a birth announcement you should not feel obligated to send them a gift. Even if a shower is given, gifts need not be elaborate or expensive.

Gifts for the Child

Parents' views on child-raising are often reflected in the gifts they choose to give or not to give to their offsprings. Some parents are of the opinion that over-indulging a child's whims will create the spoiled brat character. Others firmly believe that denying children even the smallest item will cause them to resent their parents.

I want to stress that this book is not meant to tell you what is correct to buy for your child. Every parent and child has a relationship unique and uncategorical. I do, however, feel it would be helpful, without being restrictive, to consider certain realities before buying gifts for your children.

Childhood is the most impressionable time of life. At this early stage a child's undeveloped faculties should be given exercise; in the mental realm as well as the physical one. Experts in child psychology and child-rearing usually are in agreement that the gifts we give our children should:

Give them physical exercise. It is unhealthy, physically and mentally for a child to sit quietly "like a little angel" all day long. A child is usually a powerhouse of energy which should be released daily. This release is a necessity. Toys like bicycles, jump-ropes, batons, kites, kiddie pools and monkey bars are all excellent choices in this regard.

Help children use their imagination. One of the sorriest surrogate parents today is the television set. Not only does it keep children from active physical play, it also dulls the mind. When a child watches television he does not have to use his imagination. Most of the thinking and imagining is done for him by the "boob tube". Our children are reduced to passive observers. They are spectators instead of players.

A child develops his imagination by the toys he plays with. Blocks, water paints, dolls, books or just a pencil and paper will stir the often amazing imaginations of our children.

When coupled with encouragement from a caring parent these presents can make the difference between the development of a child with an inquisitive, creative mind and one who simply soaks in ideas from those around him in a passive sponge-like manner.

Foster cooperation. Children can develop their ability to co-operate with others through the games they play. Almost all games require more than one player to co-operate in a fairly orderly manner. Children can learn to take turns, to share, and most important, to receive enjoyment from the company of others. Games are an excellent way for a parent to enter his child's world in a direct manner. By playing catch, checkers or even hide and seek with your child you may obtain a closer and more immediate relationship with him.

Be age-compatible. A child's toy should be compatible with his age. This is important because an excellent toy for a seven year old may be useless to a four year old. Here is a list with toys for certain age-groups:

Four-Six Years Old
1. building toys (blocks & erector sets)
2. puppets
3. toy cranes and cars
4. dolls and doll houses
5. balls and outdoor ball games (usually five-six years old)
6. paints and clay

Seven-Nine Years Old
1. bicycle
2. ping-pong table
3. monopoly and checkers
4. football
5. microscope
6. all board games
7. stamp and coin collections

Ten-Twelve Years Old
1. musical instruments
2. books
3. gifts pertaining to favorite hobbies of the child.

Before ending this section I should say that a child's wishes should be respected. A parent should ask the child what they would like while perhaps encouraging the toys the parents themselves believe are best. The attitude of "you'll take this and you'll like it!" should be avoided.

There hasn't been anything mentioned here about the elaborate mechanized and electronic toys. These are not highly recommended because they are usually of the passive type, giving little or no exercise to the body, imagination or spirit of cooperation in our children. Although these toys are usually the most expensive, most advertised and most purchased, they are probably not the most enjoyed. Children are not concerned with price tags and often the most cherished toys may seem dull and insignificant to those of us living outside of a child's special world.

Gifts for the College Student (Dormitory)

College students living in dormitories might be the easiest of all groups to buy for. They usually need just about everything. Most of them live in small stark rooms and eat bland institutional food. Thus the two most appreciated gifts are food and room decorations.

One of the most nourishing and cherished gifts you can give a college student is a "care package" filled with fruit, cookies, nuts, cheeses and other "munchies" that are invaluable to the late-night studier. Taking a college student out to dinner is a great way to say "I care" to someone who has been subsisting on mass produced macaroni and veiny veal.

Once their stomachs are filled, college students have to study and relax in their rooms. Every college student wants to fill his or her space with objects that reflect his or her personality. Outside assistance will be welcomed, assuming you do not offend the student's taste.

Some young scholars like candles, some like prints and posters. Other popular items are the large pillows or the beloved potted plant. A little pre-buying questioning directed to the student or his friends will help key you in on the appropriate items.

There are some practical gifts which should be recommended. Bookends, blotters, pencil holders, blankets, a desk lamp and an alarm clock are excellent gifts of this type. One thing to be avoided is the expensive pen. Most students will lose it or never use it for fear of losing it.

Gifts for the Engagement Party

Traditionally only the closest of friends and relatives bring gifts to an engagement party. However, in recent years this gift-giving practice has extended to all guests and is now expected of those invited.

Engagement gifts are never sent ahead of time as in the case of wedding presents. All gifts should be given by hand to the bride-to-be.

The type of gift given in this situation is usually something for the home or for the bride's use. Seldom is anything bestowed on the couple that is specifically for the groom. This is true even if the gift is from the groom's best friend.

Some of the more common gifts given are lingerie, linens, boudoir accessories, coffee-makers, hotplates, kitchen utensils, clocks, toasters, wine glasses and evening wear. Money is usually not an appropriate or popular gift at this particular time.

Engagement gifts need not be expensive and if you are low on funds it is best to save your money for the wedding present. Engagement gifts are a magnanimous but not a mandatory expression of our affection.

Gifts for the Wedding

An extra degree of care and expense should go into the purchasing of a wedding gift. Of all the presents we give a person during his lifetime, this is perhaps the most significant.

A couple beginning married life usually needs many of the fundamental items of the home. Clocks, tools, lamps, trays, candlesticks, carving knives, carving boards, a blender, a radio, an orange-juice maker and a coffee pot fall into this category. I would recommend these practical gifts over sentimental offerings which would not really be helpful in "setting up house."

I would also suggest monetary and utilitarian gifts for this occasion. A check or bond is a useful and thoughtful gift in the sense that it allows the couple to spend the money as they see fit. Even the closest of friends and relatives should not be hesitant about giving money to the newlyweds.

Wedding gifts should be sent ahead of time. If you send a gift after the wedding, it is proper to enclose a note explaining the reason for the gift's lateness.

A fairly popular gift-giving practice involves buying china and silverware. Often the pattern of these sets will be registered by the bride-to-be at a particular store. A guest may then purchase a piece or two from the silverware or the china set. (*See questions & answers #29.*)

Gifts for the Convalescent

Buying a gift for an ill friend or relative can be extremely difficult. There is little of the festivity and joy here that is usually part of the gift-giving experience.

Often in a hospital room we see a patient surrounded by beautiful displays of cut flowers but with nothing to do but vegetate and ponder his or her condition. Flowers do help brighten the institutional atmosphere of a hospital, but they are not a panacea for the loneliness and boredom of a hospital stay.

A thoughtful gift for someone not completely incapacitated is one which will busy their hands and minds. Books and magazines are always welcome. It is not uncommon for a patient to pass the time by sewing, drawing, writing or listening to music. These pastimes help distract the mind from the pain and unhappiness of the present moment.

One safety note should be mentioned. If a patient is being given oxygen he should not be given any electrical gift or anything that may spark. This is especially important with a child in an oxygen tent. The smallest spark can cause a fire in this situation.

To select an appropriate gift for a convalescent you should have some knowledge of their condition. Can they eat solid food? Can they move their hands? Can they see? Are they tired and listless? These facts will prevent you from buying a diary for someone whose arm is broken or a picture for someone whose eyes are bandaged. Using a few facts and a little thoughtfulness you can find a gift that may ease the sadness of this unfortunate friend or relative.

Gifts for the Wedding Anniversary

There is little advice to be given to those who bestow gifts on the anniversary of a wedding. Most married people are happy just to have their spouse remember the day. Any gift is secondary to the fact that their partner still cares enough to mark this date as a special one.

In the United States a custom which is occasionally practiced is that of giving a specific type of gift for each anniversary year. Certain anniversaries and the gifts which traditionally mark them are given below.

First	Paper
Second	Cotton or straw
Third	Leather
Fourth	Fruits, flowers, books
Fifth	Wooden
Sixth	Candy
Seventh	Woolen
Eighth	Pottery, bronze
Ninth	Willow, straw
Tenth	Tin
Twelfth	Silk
Fifteenth	Crystal
Twentieth	China
Twenty-fifth	Silver
Thirtieth	Pearl
Fortieth	Ruby, emerald
Fiftieth	Gold
Sixtieth	Diamond

Gifts for the Elderly

There has been a change in the popular conception of the older generation. Older people are not to be classified as rickety has-beens living out their last years on memories and Geritol, but as equal human beings entitled to enjoy active, useful lives, just as their children and grandchildren do.

I am not recommending that you buy a football uniform for grandpa or a tennis racket for grandma, but I'm sure there are some elderly people who *would* prefer these gifts to another teapot or picture album.

It is true that some elderly people are physically unable to indulge in many activities. Gifts for these people should be ones of comfort. Warm quilts, bathrobes and backrests will be appreciated. The more sedentary may also enjoy a record album, books or something to beautify their home.

Many older people though, have finally found the time to indulge in hobbies that the labors of youth made impossible. These hobbies such as gardening, painting, bird-watching and fishing should be encouraged by the gifts we bring.

If we know some facts, if we know the health and outlook of the person and some of the likes and dislikes, and if we combine this with thoughtfulness we can help the elders of our country enjoy the present and not simply dwell on the past happiness of their lives. Life at eighty can be just as full as life at eighteen. The gifts we give should try to stress this idea.

Gifts: Symbolic or Practical

Gift-giving might be made simpler if we placed gifts into the categories of PRACTICAL GIFTS and SYMBOLIC GIFTS.

A practical gift is an item which will prove helpful in the day-to-day activities of life. A toaster, a tablecloth, a crockpot or a can-opener is a practical present. These articles are especially well-received by those who have a true need for them. Newly-weds, home-buyers, college students and generally anybody lacking some of these necessities are all excellent candidates for the practical gift.

It is, however, wasteful and redundant to buy a coffee-maker for a family that probably has one too many. If a person is having trouble storing all the extra dishes in his possession, why buy him additional ones? If the person we are buying for is very comfortable financially, it might be better to avoid the practical gift. These people have the necessary funds and may prefer choosing precisely the type of radio, rotisserie or iron they want.

The alternative to the practical gift is the symbolic one. A purely symbolic gift excels in sentimental value but really has no utilitarian function. These are by far the most enjoyable gifts to give and may prove the most cherished by the receiver. Probably the world's most popular symbolic gift is the flower. No matter how expensive roses become, millions are sent on Valentine's Day and every other day of the year. The flower is the perfect symbol of natural beauty and elegance. Even the brevity of its bloom adds to its charm.

Jewelry is an extremely popular symbolic token, among which the diamond engagement ring reigns supreme. Here again nature has provided a symbol to mirror human emotion. The beauty and durability of the diamond reflects the enduring and precious nature of the bond between the engaged couple. Gold, too, is symbolic of the strong and untarnished affection one person has for another.

People often enjoy novel gifts which represent something important in their lives. People with a musical background will probably appreciate a statue, a book, a picture or any item with a musical theme. The same approach applies to those who love sports, horses or a particular part of the world. Even though these gifts will not help cook dinner or clean house, they can bring great joy if they are chosen with the recipient's tastes in mind.

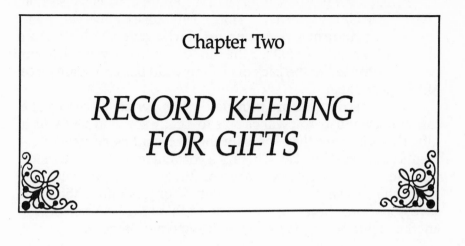

Chapter Two

RECORD KEEPING FOR GIFTS

"Giving requires good sense."

—Ovid

How to Keep Gift Records

In this part of the book you will be able to enter information about gifts received and given. The section "Records of Gifts Given" has a column for the date, the occasion, who you are giving the gift to, a description of the gift, the cost of the gift, where the gift was purchased, and whether you have received a thank-you note for the gift.

The uses of "Record of Gifts Given" are numerous. You will know the gifts you have given to a person and will not make the mistake of giving the same gift twice. If a person you have given a gift later tells you he wishes to return it, you can provide him with the date and place of purchase. The "acknowledgement received" column may prove useful if you mail a gift. When an acknowledgement is not received after a month or two it might indicate that the gift was never received. You can then inquire to see if the gift was possibly lost in the mail.

The section headed "Record of Gifts Received" provides a space for entry of the date, the person(s) from whom you received a gift, a description of the gift, the occasion, and whether or not you have sent an acknowledgement.

Perhaps the most useful part of the entire book is the section "Record of Gifts Received". How many times have you gone through the chore of making up a list of who gave which gift at an affair. This list is essential for the sending of thank-you notes but is often entrusted to the back of an empty gift box or a spare piece of looseleaf paper.

In this section you are provided with a perfect place to make this important list. You will be able to clearly see who sent which gift. This will make the confusing chore of sending acknowledgements easier and quicker. There is a convenient column in which you can mark whether you have or have not sent a thank-you note. The compact and organized entry of this information can save you from the embarrassment of thanking one person for another's gift or forgetting to thank someone altogether.

Gifts Given

Given To	Date	Description of Gift	Occasion	Cost	Where Bought	Acknowledgement Received

Gifts Given

Given To	Date	Description of Gift	Occasion	Cost	Where Bought	Acknowledgement Received

Gifts Given

Given To	Date	Description of Gift	Occasion	Cost	Where Bought	Acknowledgement Received

Gifts Given

Given To	Date	Description of Gift	Occasion	Cost	Where Bought	Acknowledgement Received

Gifts Given

Given To	Date	Description of Gift	Occasion	Cost	Where Bought	Acknowledgement Received

Gifts Given

Given To	Date	Description of Gift	Occasion	Cost	Where Bought	Acknowledgement Received

Gifts Given

Given To	Date	Description of Gift	Occasion	Cost	Where Bought	Acknowledgement Received

Gifts Given

Given To	Date	Description of Gift	Occasion	Cost	Where Bought	Acknowledgement Received

Gifts Given

Given To	Date	Description of Gift	Occasion	Cost	Where Bought	Acknowledgement Received

Gifts Given

Given To	Date	Description of Gift	Occasion	Cost	Where Bought	Acknowledgement Received

Gifts Given

Given To	Date	Description of Gift	Occasion	Cost	Where Bought	Acknowledgement Received

Gifts Given

Given To	Date	Description of Gift	Occasion	Cost	Where Bought	Acknowledgement Received

Gifts Given

Given To	Date	Description of Gift	Occasion	Cost	Where Bought	Acknowledgement Received

Gifts Given

Given To	Date	Description of Gift	Occasion	Cost	Where Bought	Acknowledgement Received

Gifts Given

Given To	Date	Description of Gift	Occasion	Cost	Where Bought	Acknowledgement Received

Gifts Given

Given To	Date	Description of Gift	Occasion	Cost	Where Bought	Acknowledgement Received

Gifts Given

Given To	Date	Description of Gift	Occasion	Cost	Where Bought	Acknowledgement Received

Gifts Given

Given To	Date	Description of Gift	Occasion	Cost	Where Bought	Acknowledgement Received

Gifts Given

Given To	Date	Description of Gift	Occasion	Cost	Where Bought	Acknowledgement Received

Gifts Given

Given To	Date	Description of Gift	Occasion	Cost	Where Bought	Acknowledgement Received

Gifts Given

Given To	Date	Description of Gift	Occasion	Cost	Where Bought	Acknowledgement Received

Gifts Given

Given To	Date	Description of Gift	Occasion	Cost	Where Bought	Acknowledgement Received

Gifts Given

Given To	Date	Description of Gift	Occasion	Cost	Where Bought	Acknowledgement Received

Gifts Given

Given To	Date	Description of Gift	Occasion	Cost	Where Bought	Acknowledgement Received

Gifts Given

Given To	Date	Description of Gift	Occasion	Cost	Where Bought	Acknowledgement Received

Gifts Given

Given To	Date	Description of Gift	Occasion	Cost	Where Bought	Acknowledgement Received

Gifts Given

Given To	Date	Description of Gift	Occasion	Cost	Where Bought	Acknowledgement Received

Gifts Received

Received From	Date	Description of Gift	Occasion	Acknowledgement Sent

Gifts Received

Received From	Date	Description of Gift	Occasion	Acknowledgement Sent

Gifts Received

Received From	Date	Description of Gift	Occasion	Acknowledgement Sent

Gifts Received

Received From	Date	Description of Gift	Occasion	Acknowledgement Sent

Gifts Received

Received From	Date	Description of Gift	Occasion	Acknowledgement Sent

Gifts Received

Received From	Date	Description of Gift	Occasion	Acknowledgement Sent

Gifts Received

Received From	Date	Description of Gift	Occasion	Acknowledgement Sent

Gifts Received

Received From	Date	Description of Gift	Occasion	Acknowledgement Sent

Gifts Received

Received From	Date	Description of Gift	Occasion	Acknowledgement Sent

Gifts Received

Received From	Date	Description of Gift	Occasion	Acknowledgement Sent

Gifts Received

Received From	Date	Description of Gift	Occasion	Acknowledgement Sent

Gifts Received

Received From	Date	Description of Gift	Occasion	Acknowledgement Sent

Gifts Received

Received From	Date	Description of Gift	Occasion	Acknowledgement Sent

Gifts Received

Received From	Date	Description of Gift	Occasion	Acknowledgement Sent

Gifts Received

Received From	Date	Description of Gift	Occasion	Acknowledgement Sent

Gifts Received

Received From	Date	Description of Gift	Occasion	Acknowledgement Sent

Gifts Received

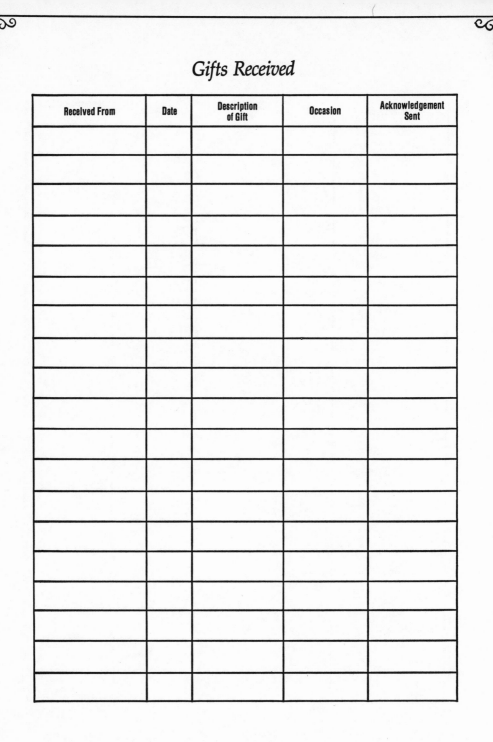

Received From	Date	Description of Gift	Occasion	Acknowledgement Sent

Gifts Received

Received From	Date	Description of Gift	Occasion	Acknowledgement Sent

Gifts Received

Received From	Date	Description of Gift	Occasion	Acknowledgement Sent

Gifts Received

Received From	Date	Description of Gift	Occasion	Acknowledgement Sent

Gifts Received

Received From	Date	Description of Gift	Occasion	Acknowledgement Sent

Gifts Received

Received From	Date	Description of Gift	Occasion	Acknowledgement Sent

Gifts Received

Received From	Date	Description of Gift	Occasion	Acknowledgement Sent

Gifts Received

Received From	Date	Description of Gift	Occasion	Acknowledgement Sent

Gifts Received

Received From	Date	Description of Gift	Occasion	Acknowledgement Sent

Received From	Date	Description of Gift	Occasion	Acknowledgement Sent

Gifts Received

Received From	Date	Description of Gift	Occasion	Acknowledgement Sent

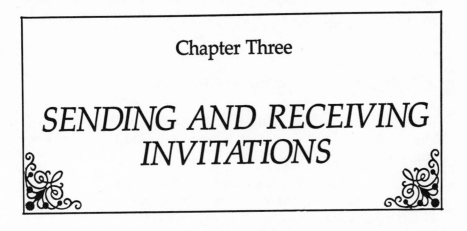

Chapter Three

SENDING AND RECEIVING INVITATIONS

"But as they were all sitting down to dinner, they saw coming into the hall an old Fairy, whom they had not invited— she said the Princess should have her hand pierced with a spindle and die."
—*Sleeping Beauty*

Introduction to Invitations

There are a number of courtesies and traditions concerning the sending and receiving of invitations. Although many people feel these "rules" of etiquette are antiquated, there is a large part of the population that tries to comply with them.

In the following section I will review some of the basic rules in this area and hopefully answer any questions you may have about the subject.

An invitation functions in two ways. Primarily it is a manner of informing someone that you are having a gathering and that you request their attendance. You are informing them of when and where the occasion is to take place.

In addition to this service, the invitation sets the tone of your affair. A convenient way to divide social occasions is into three groups: formal, semi-formal and informal. The invitation to each of these types of gatherings should reflect the mood of the occasion. We will examine each of these categories and explain what an invitation to each should and should not include.

Formal Invitations

Formal invitations are sent when you are having an official luncheon, a formal dinner or a wedding. The following rules apply to this type of invitation:

1. The invitation is always written in the third person.
2. The invitation is sent at least two weeks before the affair (four to six weeks ahead in the case of a wedding).
3. The invitation never has a telephone number written or printed on it.
4. The invitation is engraved, printed or hand-written on plain white paper.*

EXAMPLE:

Mr. and Mrs. Robert Updike
request the company of
Dr. and Mrs. Johnson at dinner
on Friday, June the seventeenth
at eight o'clock

422 Madison Avenue
R.S.V.P.   *New York, New York 10012*

---

*Wedding invitations of the formal type are almost always engraved. We will not discuss the printed forms of invitations here. Any competent printer is well aware of these forms and to deal with them here would be redundant.

In replying to these invitations we should be prompt. Arrangements have to be made by the host or hostess and these will depend on how many people will be attending. A formal invitation requires a formal reply written in the third person on plain white paper.

EXAMPLE OF FORMAL ACCEPTANCE:

Mr. and Mrs. Donald Lovejoy
accept with pleasure
the kind invitation of
Mr. and Mrs. William Jones Johnson, Jr.
for dinner
on Monday the tenth of December
at half past eight o'clock

Sometimes an invitation will include a reply card. In these situations the card should be returned as soon as possible.

Semiformal Invitations

Semiformal affairs are perhaps the most difficult to define. Drawing the line between formal and semiformal is fairly arbitrary as is the distinction between semiformal and informal. Let us call a semiformal occasion one in which there is not the rigid necessity of formal evening attire and table settings, yet an affair with some degree of adherence to social convention in dress and manners. Examples of these affairs are the small dinner party, the afternoon tea and the informal dance. However, any type of affair can be set in the semiformal mode.

Semiformal invitations can be written on a person's visiting card if they have one. A visiting card is a small white card with a person's name printed in the middle and the address printed in the lower right hand corner.

EXAMPLES OF INVITATIONS WRITTEN ON VISITING CARD:

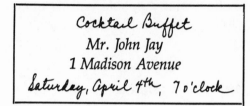

> *Cocktail Buffet*
> Mr. John Jay
> 1 Madison Avenue
> *Saturday, April 4th, 7 o'clock*

> *Tea*
> Mrs. Ann Bowlin
> 1150 Park Avenue
> *Monday, June 17th, 2 o'clock*

Semiformal invitations may also be written on folding cards with or without the host or hostess's name engraved on them. If the name is engraved on the card the invitation may be written in this manner:

> *Cocktail Buffet*
> Mrs. Mary Alberts
> *Tuesday, April 9th, 2:30 o'clock*
> *9 Cherry Lane*

If you do not have engraved folding cards and do not wish to go to the expense and trouble of having them printed, it is perfectly acceptable to write a short note on a blank white folding card.

EXAMPLE:

> Dear Jane, June 17
>
> Should you and Bob be able to join us for dinner on Friday, June 30th?
>
> Anna Jones
>
> 18 Hudson Ave.

When replying to this type of invitation you should telephone or write a short informal note. Some invitations will have the words "regrets only" on them. In these cases there is a necessity to reply only if you will not be attending the affair.

Informal Invitations

Most gatherings held today are informal in nature. Cocktail parties, birthdays, anniversaries, showers, dances and luncheons are often set in a casual mode and the invitation reflects this.

Informal invitations can be extended by telephone or by writing. If you choose to invite by telephone you simply call the person or couple you are inviting and inform them when and where the party will take place. It is often wise to send a reminder card to these people as the occasion nears.

If you decide to send written invitations, you may choose one of the myriad colorful, illustrated cards printed for each particular occasion. These cards are usually of the fill-in type (e.g., you fill in where, when, etc.) and include your telephone number on the invitation. Or be creative and design your own cards. There is very little that you cannot do regarding invitations of this type. As long as you are sure to give the necessary information, these invitations may take just about any form you choose for them.

Chapter Four

RECORD KEEPING FOR INVITATIONS

Introduction to Invitation Forms

This section of the book provides you with pages on which to keep records of invitations you send and receive. The form "Invitations Received" specifies who the invitation was received from, when it was received, the date of the occasion, when you sent your reply, and the gift you gave.

In addition there are spaces to briefly describe the type and attire of the affair.

The form "Record of Invitations Given" provides space for a description of the type of invitation sent, who you sent it to, the date of the occasion, whether you received an acceptance, and the type of gift received.

There are numerous practical advantages to keeping both these records. "Invitations Received" will provide you with a convenient reminder of just when an occasion is or was, whether or not you have given the required reply and just what you gave your friend or relative on some past occasion. This section may also prove to be a bit of memorabilia as you recall brief descriptions of each of the many occasions in your lifetime.

The section "Invitations Given" is invaluable in the planning of an affair. It gives you a complete listing of guests invited, whether they have replied as yet and whether you have acknowledged their gift with a thank-you note.

Invitations Received

Received From	Date Received	Date of Occasion	Type of Occasion	Date Accepted	Attire	Gift

Invitations Received

Received From	Date Received	Date of Occasion	Type of Occasion	Date Accepted	Attire	Gift

Invitations Received

Received From	Date Received	Date of Occasion	Type of Occasion	Date Accepted	Attire	Gift

Invitations Received

Received From	Date Received	Date of Occasion	Type of Occasion	Date Accepted	Attire	Gift

Invitations Received

Received From	Date Received	Date of Occasion	Type of Occasion	Date Accepted	Attire	Gift

Invitations Received

Received From	Date Received	Date of Occasion	Type of Occasion	Date Accepted	Attire	Gift

Invitations Received

Received From	Date Received	Date of Occasion	Type of Occasion	Date Accepted	Attire	Gift

Invitations Received

Received From	Date Received	Date of Occasion	Type of Occasion	Date Accepted	Attire	Gift

Invitations Received

Received From	Date Received	Date of Occasion	Type of Occasion	Date Accepted	Attire	Gift

Invitations Received

Received From	Date Received	Date of Occasion	Type of Occasion	Date Accepted	Attire	Gift

Invitations Received

Received From	Date Received	Date of Occasion	Type of Occasion	Date Accepted	Attire	Gift

Invitations Received

Received From	Date Received	Date of Occasion	Type of Occasion	Date Accepted	Attire	Gift

Invitations Received

Received From	Date Received	Date of Occasion	Type of Occasion	Date Accepted	Attire	Gift

Invitations Received

Received From	Date Received	Date of Occasion	Type of Occasion	Date Accepted	Attire	Gift

Invitations Received

Received From	Date Received	Date of Occasion	Type of Occasion	Date Accepted	Attire	Gift

Invitations Received

Received From	Date Received	Date of Occasion	Type of Occasion	Date Accepted	Attire	Gift

Invitations Received

Received From	Date Received	Date of Occasion	Type of Occasion	Date Accepted	Attire	Gift

Invitations Received

Received From	Date Received	Date of Occasion	Type of Occasion	Date Accepted	Attire	Gift

Invitations Received

Received From	Date Received	Date of Occasion	Type of Occasion	Date Accepted	Attire	Gift

Invitations Received

Received From	Date Received	Date of Occasion	Type of Occasion	Date Accepted	Attire	Gift

Invitations Received

Received From	Date Received	Date of Occasion	Type of Occasion	Date Accepted	Attire	Gift

Invitations Received

Received From	Date Received	Date of Occasion	Type of Occasion	Date Accepted	Attire	Gift

Invitations Received

Received From	Date Received	Date of Occasion	Type of Occasion	Date Accepted	Attire	Gift

Invitations Received

Received From	Date Received	Date of Occasion	Type of Occasion	Date Accepted	Attire	Gift

Invitations Received

Received From	Date Received	Date of Occasion	Type of Occasion	Date Accepted	Attire	Gift

Invitations Received

Received From	Date Received	Date of Occasion	Type of Occasion	Date Accepted	Attire	Gift

Invitations Extended

Name of Invitee	Date Extended	Date of Occasion	Type of Occasion	Acceptance Received	Gift Received

Invitations Extended

Name of Invitee	Date Extended	Date of Occasion	Type of Occasion	Acceptance Received	Gift Received

Invitations Extended

Name of Invitee	Date Extended	Date of Occasion	Type of Occasion	Acceptance Received	Gift Received

Invitations Extended

Name of Invitee	Date Extended	Date of Occasion	Type of Occasion	Acceptance Received	Gift Received

Invitations Extended

Name of Invitee	Date Extended	Date of Occasion	Type of Occasion	Acceptance Received	Gift Received

Invitations Extended

Name of Invitee	Date Extended	Date of Occasion	Type of Occasion	Acceptance Received	Gift Received

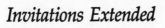

Invitations Extended

Name of Invitee	Date Extended	Date of Occasion	Type of Occasion	Acceptance Received	Gift Received

Invitations Extended

Name of Invitee	Date Extended	Date of Occasion	Type of Occasion	Acceptance Received	Gift Received

Invitations Extended

Name of Invitee	Date Extended	Date of Occasion	Type of Occasion	Acceptance Received	Gift Received

Invitations Extended

Name of Invitee	Date Extended	Date of Occasion	Type of Occasion	Acceptance Received	Gift Received

Invitations Extended

Name of Invitee	Date Extended	Date of Occasion	Type of Occasion	Acceptance Received	Gift Received

Invitations Extended

Name of Invitee	Date Extended	Date of Occasion	Type of Occasion	Acceptance Received	Gift Received

Invitations Extended

Name of Invitee	Date Extended	Date of Occasion	Type of Occasion	Acceptance Received	Gift Received

Invitations Extended

Name of Invitee	Date Extended	Date of Occasion	Type of Occasion	Acceptance Received	Gift Received

Invitations Extended

Name of Invitee	Date Extended	Date of Occasion	Type of Occasion	Acceptance Received	Gift Received

Invitations Extended

Name of Invitee	Date Extended	Date of Occasion	Type of Occasion	Acceptance Received	Gift Received

Name of Invitee	Date Extended	Date of Occasion	Type of Occasion	Acceptance Received	Gift Received

Invitations Extended

Name of Invitee	Date Extended	Date of Occasion	Type of Occasion	Acceptance Received	Gift Received

Name of Invitee	Date Extended	Date of Occasion	Type of Occasion	Acceptance Received	Gift Received

Invitations Extended

Name of Invitee	Date Extended	Date of Occasion	Type of Occasion	Acceptance Received	Gift Received

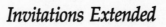

Invitations Extended

Name of Invitee	Date Extended	Date of Occasion	Type of Occasion	Acceptance Received	Gift Received

Invitations Extended

Name of Invitee	Date Extended	Date of Occasion	Type of Occasion	Acceptance Received	Gift Received

Invitations Extended

Name of Invitee	Date Extended	Date of Occasion	Type of Occasion	Acceptance Received	Gift Received

Chapter Five

THIRTY VITAL QUESTIONS AND ANSWERS ABOUT GIFTS AND INVITATIONS

Questions & Answers

1. **Q:** Which occasions do not require gifts from those invited?

   A: Gifts are not necessary when attending dinner parties or luncheons. In addition, any invitation one receives that states "No Gifts Please" should be complied with. At a christening only the immediate family is expected to bring gifts. Confirmation ceremonies do not require gifts although guests very close to the family often bring some religious token. Engagement parties do not require gifts although it is becoming commonplace to give them at these occasions. (*See Gifts for the Engagement Party.*)

2. **Q:** When is it improper to give a cash gift to someone?

   A: There are very few times money is not appreciated as a gift. Whether in the form of cash, a gift certificate or a savings bond, money is useful and welcome. Usually money is given at weddings, bar-mitzvahs and graduations as opposed to bridal showers, birthday parties and farewell gatherings. You must use your discretion. If you know a person or a couple in desperate need of funds, money might be the most appropriate gift on any occasion.

3. **Q:** Should thank-you notes be sent for any gift received or

just for those received on special occasions?

A: Thank-you notes are not mandatory (although often sent) when you have already thanked someone personally for a gift they have given you by hand. If a gift is sent ahead (e.g., a wedding gift) it becomes mandatory to send a thank-you note.

4. **Q:** At any engagement party should the gift be for the bride, the groom or both?

A: Engagement gifts have traditionally been for the bride. The present practice, however, is to buy something which both parties can make use of. (*See Gifts for the Engagement Party.*)

5. **Q:** Should the wedding gift be for the bride, the groom or both?

A: Wedding gifts have traditionally been for both participants. One should not give a gift that is obviously useful to one partner and not the other (e.g., lipstick holder, after-shave kit.)

6. **Q:** If an engagement is broken after the engagement party should all the gifts be returned?

A: Yes. All gifts should be returned with a short note enclosed telling why the gift is being returned.

7. **Q:** If a marriage breaks up within six months of the wedding should the wedding gifts be returned?

A: No. Marriage gifts are never returned after the wedding, even if the marriage lasts one day. Marriage gifts sent before the wedding should be returned if the marriage ceremony is called off.

8. **Q:** When you do not receive a gift from someone is it proper to ask them about it?

A: If you do not receive a gift and suspect that it was lost in the mail you might be tempted to inquire about it. This is a delicate situation because if you confront someone with this question and they did not send you a gift, you will embarrass them. On the other hand, if they did send you a gift they will never know that it was lost unless you tell them that you never received it.

The most tactful thing to do is not mention it. The gift-giver will eventually inquire how you are enjoying his gift (if he indeed sent one) and at this time you can mention that you never received it.

9. **Q:** Is it possible that an extremely expensive gift could be the wrong choice?

A: Yes. You should never give someone a gift that is not suited to their lifestyle. It would be insensitive to give solid gold candlesticks to someone who cannot afford silverware or to give a Tiffany lamp to someone who furnishes his home in an inexpensive manner. In addition to being out of place and useless, these gifts put the recipient in a position of being unable to reciprocate the gesture with a gift of equal worth.

10. **Q:** How soon after receiving a gift should thank-you notes be sent?

A: Thank-you notes should be sent as soon as possible after the affair takes place. If there is not an affair, they should be sent as soon as the gift is received. They should always be hand-written even if this takes more time and labor.

11. **Q:** When is it unwise to buy jewelry as a gift?

A: Jewelry is a difficult and costly gift to buy in most cases. First one should realize that you are dealing with something someone else must wear. You must take into account the taste of the recipient. If you are not aware of their preferences in this area do not buy them jewelry.

Jewelry is also a symbolic gift in many instances (*See Gifts: Symbolic or Practical*) and you should be careful that the gift you give is a proper reflection of the relationship you have with someone. It is unwise to give jewels to the wives of friends if you are a man, or to the husbands of friends, if you are a woman. Your friend might object to seeing his partner wearing jewelry from another, even if the gift has been given with the most platonic thoughts in mind.

Jewelry is often a personal and special gift, not to be given or taken lightly. There is often a romantic association, as jewelry often symbolizes deep love and affection.

12. **Q:** When is it unwise to buy clothes as a gift?

A: If jewelry is difficult to buy for someone, clothes are almost impossible. In this case you must know the recipient's tastes very well. You must also know the right size. If you are aware of both these things you should still only buy clothes which are not extremely expensive or faddish. Stay away from hats, as people are particularly choosey about them. All things considered it seems people enjoy choosing their own clothes and should be allowed to do so. I would think that a gift certificate to someone's favorite department store would be preferable to a gift of clothes.

13. **Q:** Should a receipt ever be enclosed with a gift in case the recipient should care to return the gift?

    A: No. If you want to make it easier for someone to return a gift just make sure to place the gift in a box with the name of the store from which it was purchased. Most department stores and gift shops have their own boxes.

14. **Q:** If an engagement is broken should the woman return the engagement ring?

    A: Yes. No matter who breaks the engagement it is necessary for the woman to return the engagement ring. An engagement is a trial period and if the engagement is terminated the woman has no reason to keep the ring.

15. **Q:** At a wedding should gifts be handed to the bride or the groom?

    A: Wedding gifts should be sent ahead. However if they are brought to the affair they should be placed on a table provided for them. If a check is brought it should be presented to the bride.

16. **Q:** What types of gifts can be ordered and sent by mail?

    A: The lazy gift buyer is in luck today. Almost anything that can be bought in a store can be bought by mail and sent in the same manner. Flowers, candy, gift certificates or any gift from the numerous gift catalogues can be sent without even leaving your home. Most large department stores have gift catalogues displaying a wide variety of gifts and will mail them anywhere in the world.

17. **Q:** If you do not attend a wedding you are invited to should you send a gift?

    A: You are not obligated to send a gift if you do not attend. Many people do send a gift, but this is a matter of personal preference and not an obligation.

18. **Q:** Is it proper to invite a relative without inviting his children?

    A: Yes. Often a wedding list is restricted in number and children must be left out.

19. **Q:** Is it proper to invite a husband without his wife, or vice versa?

    A: No. The only time when a man or woman is invited without their partner is when the affair itself applies to only one gender (e.g., woman's luncheon, men's club gathering, etc.). But at any affair to which couples are invited it is unthinkable to invite one spouse and not the other.

20. **Q:** Should you bother sending invitations to people who live so far away you are sure they will not attend the affair?

    A: It is best to send these people wedding announcements. This way they feel no obligation to send a gift yet they do not feel forgotten.

21. **Q:** Is it proper to invite to your wedding every couple that invited you or your spouse to theirs?

    A: No. It is not expected. The people that invited you may have had a large wedding while yours may be small.

22. **Q:** Is it proper to state the dress code for a party on an invitation?

    A: Yes. Today most parties are informal so it is necessary to write "black-tie" on the invitation if you require formal attire. To be safe it might be wise to write "informal" on invitations to this type of gathering so that guests will not have any apprehension about leaving their ties and gowns at home.

23. **Q:** If you do not receive a response call from someone you sent an invitation to is it polite to call and ask them if they are coming?

    A: Yes. If you do not receive your requested reply and the affair is approaching you may call or write the invited guest and inquire whether they will be attending.

24. **Q:** If you receive an invitation that does not indicate that a reply is necessary should you inform the host and hostess whether you are coming or not?

A: It is not mandatory but it is advisable and appreciated.

25. **Q:** What are the gifts traditionally associated with each of the anniversaries?

A: See "Gifts for the Wedding Anniversary."

26. **Q:** Which gifts are tax deductible?

A: Gifts given to charitable organization are tax deductible. Salvation Army donations, contributions to cancer research, children's foundations and cultural societies all fall into this category.

27. **Q:** Is it wise to buy toys for other people's children?

A: The best rule to follow in this case is to ask the parents. Many parents are very particular about the kind of toys they want their children to play with. (*See Gifts for the Child.*)

28. **Q:** When one wants to register a pattern for dishes, glassware or silverware in a store how does one go about doing it?

A: All that is required is for the bride and groom to go to the store and choose the patterns they want. This should be done well in advance of the wedding. People will ask the bride or groom what they would like for a wedding gift and they will be informed that the couple is registered with a particular store. The future guest can either telephone or visit the store and choose some article that he can afford.

The bride and groom have the option, at some stores, of having each piece of china or silverware mailed to them as they are bought or having all the pieces held at the store until after the wedding. This second option allows the bride and groom to exchange one item for another if they feel this is necessary. For instance, if the table settings are incomplete the couple can sacrifice a salad bowl and use the credit to complete the set.

29. **Q:** When is it proper to request a particular gift?

A: If you are registered with a certain store you may tell someone this. Otherwise it is best to be vague when someone asks you what they can get you. You do not want to force someone into buying something they cannot afford and asking for too specific a gift can do just that. You could simply imply that you would like something for the kitchen, the garden, the walls of your home, etc. This answers the question without cornering anybody.

30. **Q:** Is it always necessary to wrap a gift?

A: No. Christmas gifts are usually wrapped, but other gifts need not be. Most stores have fairly decorative boxes with the store's emblem on them. These require no wrapping. Obviously, if a gift is in an unsightly cardboard box or crate it should be wrapped.

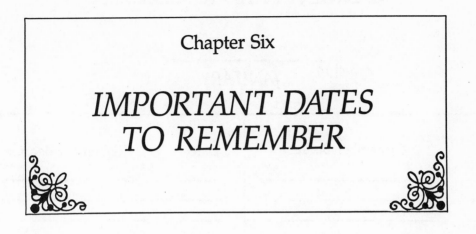

Chapter Six

IMPORTANT DATES TO REMEMBER

Use the pages in this section to annotate important dates to remember, such as, ANNIVERSARIES, BIRTHDAYS, DUE DATES, FINANCIAL INCOME DATES, SPECIAL OCCASIONS, SOCIAL, etc.

IMPORTANT DATES TO REMEMBER

JANUARY

Date	Remember Because	Date	Remember Because

IMPORTANT DATES TO REMEMBER

JANUARY

Date	Remember Because	Date	Remember Because

IMPORTANT DATES TO REMEMBER

FEBRUARY

Date	Remember Because	Date	Remember Because

IMPORTANT DATES TO REMEMBER

_____

FEBRUARY

Date	Remember Because	Date	Remember Because

IMPORTANT DATES TO REMEMBER

MARCH

Date	Remember Because	Date	Remember Because

IMPORTANT DATES TO REMEMBER

MARCH

Date	Remember Because	Date	Remember Because

IMPORTANT DATES TO REMEMBER

APRIL

Date	Remember Because	Date	Remember Because

IMPORTANT DATES TO REMEMBER

APRIL

Date	Remember Because	Date	Remember Because

IMPORTANT DATES TO REMEMBER

MAY

Date	Remember Because	Date	Remember Because

IMPORTANT DATES TO REMEMBER

_____

MALY

Date	Remember Because	Date	Remember Because

IMPORTANT DATES TO REMEMBER

JUNE

Date	Remember Because	Date	Remember Because

IMPORTANT DATES TO REMEMBER

JUNE

Date	Remember Because	Date	Remember Because

IMPORTANT DATES TO REMEMBER

JULY

Date	Remember Because	Date	Remember Because
___	_____	___	_____
___	_____	___	_____
___	_____	___	_____
___	_____	___	_____
___	_____	___	_____
___	_____	___	_____
___	_____	___	_____
___	_____	___	_____
___	_____	___	_____
___	_____	___	_____
___	_____	___	_____
___	_____	___	_____
___	_____	___	_____
___	_____	___	_____
___	_____	___	_____
___	_____	___	_____
___	_____	___	_____
___	_____	___	_____
___	_____	___	_____
___	_____	___	_____
___	_____	___	_____
___	_____	___	_____
___	_____	___	_____
___	_____	___	_____
___	_____	___	_____
___	_____	___	_____

IMPORTANT DATES TO REMEMBER

JULY

Date	Remember Because	Date	Remember Because

IMPORTANT DATES TO REMEMBER

AUGUST

Date	Remember Because	Date	Remember Because

IMPORTANT DATES TO REMEMBER

AUGUST

Date	Remember Because	Date	Remember Because

IMPORTANT DATES TO REMEMBER

SEPTEMBER

Date	Remember Because	Date	Remember Because

IMPORTANT DATES TO REMEMBER

SEPTEMBER

Date	Remember Because	Date	Remember Because

IMPORTANT DATES TO REMEMBER

OCTOBER

Date	Remember Because	Date	Remember Because

IMPORTANT DATES TO REMEMBER

OCTOBER

Date	Remember Because	Date	Remember Because

IMPORTANT DATES TO REMEMBER

NOVEMBER

Date	Remember Because	Date	Remember Because

IMPORTANT DATES TO REMEMBER

_____

NOVEMBER

Date	Remember Because	Date	Remember Because

IMPORTANT DATES TO REMEMBER

DECEMBER

Date	Remember Because	Date	Remember Because

IMPORTANT DATES TO REMEMBER

DECEMBER

Date	Remember Because	Date	Remember Because